Animals of the Desert

Roadrunner

E. Melanie Watt

AV2
www.openlightbox.com

Step 1
Go to **www.openlightbox.com**

Step 2
Enter this unique code
PIJOD4ZDA

Step 3
Explore your interactive eBook!

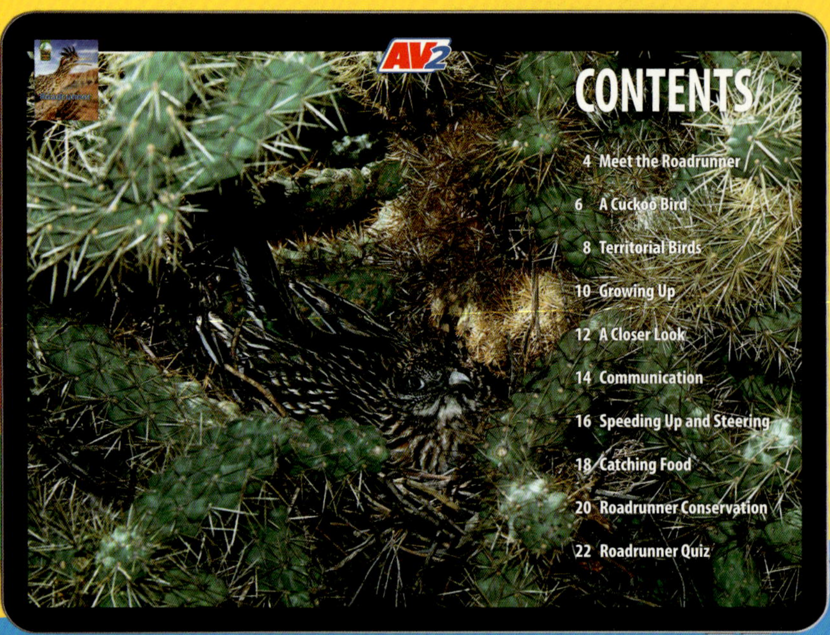

AV2 is optimized for use on any device

Your interactive eBook comes with...

Contents
Browse a live contents page to easily navigate through resources

Audio
Listen to sections of the book read aloud

Videos
Watch informative video clips

Weblinks
Gain additional information for research

Slideshows
View images and captions

Try This!
Complete activities and hands-on experiments

Key Words
Study vocabulary, and complete a matching word activity

Quizzes
Test your knowledge

Share
Share titles within your Learning Management System (LMS) or Library Circulation System

Citation
Create bibliographical references following APA, CMOS, and MLA styles

This title is part of our AV2 digital subscription

1-Year Grades K–5 Subscription
ISBN 978-1-7911-3320-7

Access hundreds of AV2 titles with our digital subscription.
Sign up for a FREE trial at **www.openlightbox.com/trial**

The digital components of this book are guaranteed to stay active for at least five years from the date of publication.

Roadrunner

CONTENTS

Meet the Roadrunner

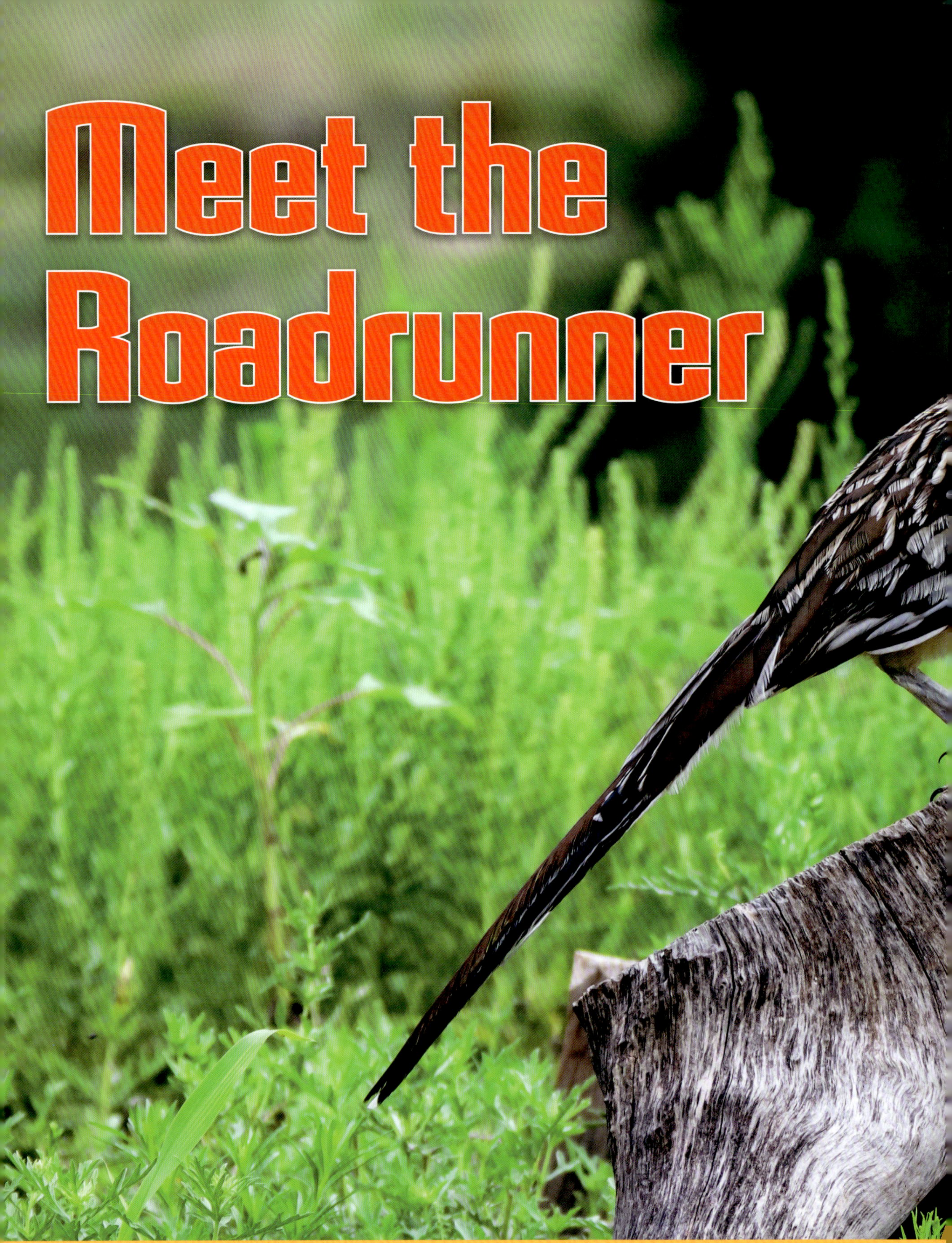

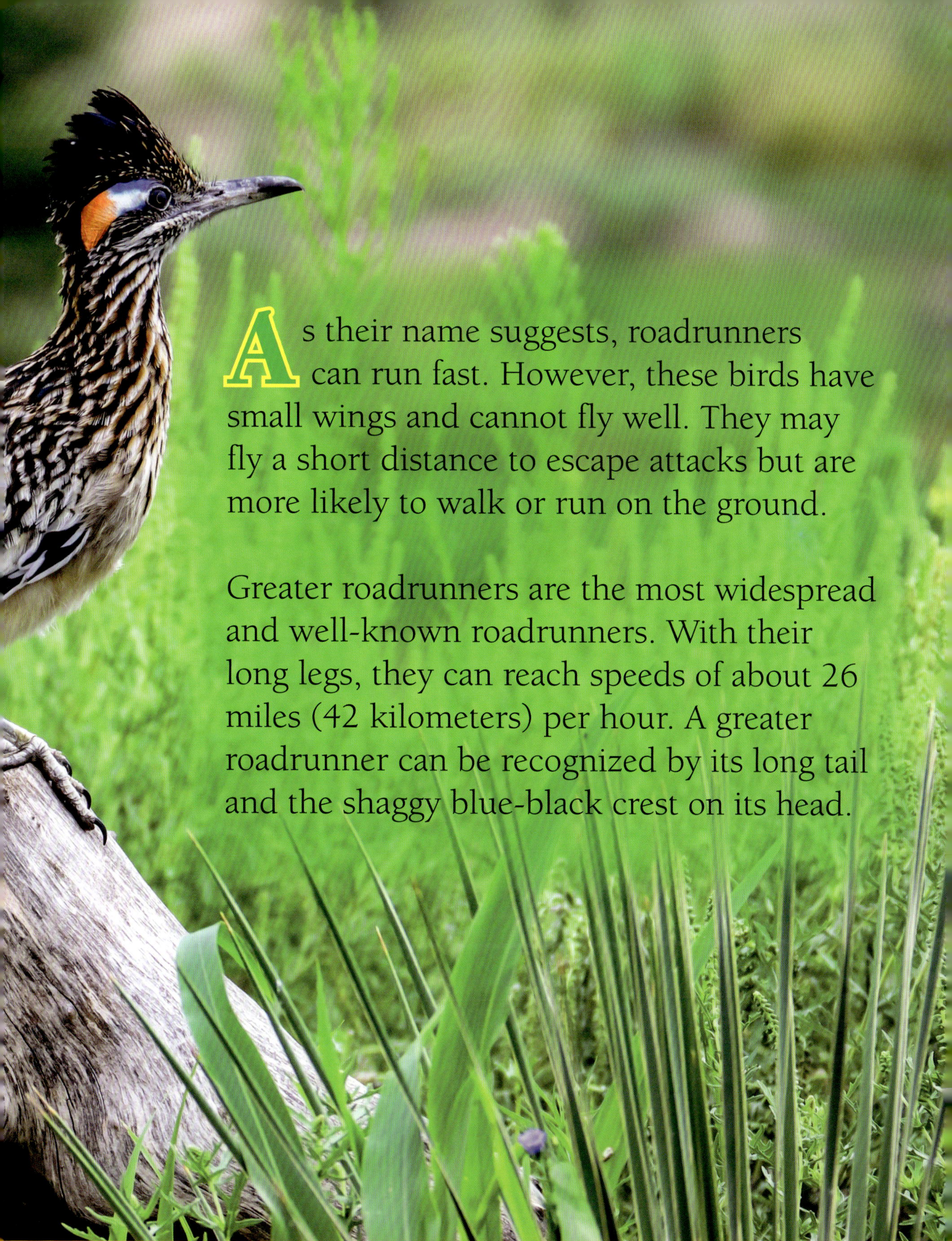

As their name suggests, roadrunners can run fast. However, these birds have small wings and cannot fly well. They may fly a short distance to escape attacks but are more likely to walk or run on the ground.

Greater roadrunners are the most widespread and well-known roadrunners. With their long legs, they can reach speeds of about 26 miles (42 kilometers) per hour. A greater roadrunner can be recognized by its long tail and the shaggy blue-black crest on its head.

A Cuckoo Bird

Roadrunners are part of the cuckoo family. There are only two roadrunner **species**. Lesser roadrunners live in **shrublands** in Mexico and Central America. They are smaller than greater roadrunners.

Greater roadrunners live in deserts, grasslands, and shrublands in Mexico and the United States. Their feathers are gray, brown, and black with white streaks. These colors help the birds blend into the environment. Greater roadrunners grow up to 24 inches (62 centimeters) long.

Weight Difference
Little Cuckoo
1.4 ounces (40 g)
Lesser Roadrunner
7 ounces (200 g)
Banded Ground Cuckoo
14 ounces (400 g)
Greater Roadrunner
19 ounces (540 g)
= 2 ounces (57 grams)

Territorial Birds

Greater roadrunners live alone or in **mated pairs**. These pairs stay together for life. They defend a **territory** that is about 0.5 miles (0.8 km) across. The birds use their territory to hunt, build nests, and raise their young.

The males make loud calls. This helps neighboring birds stay out of each other's way. If another bird does enter their land, the mated pair call loudly and rush at the invader until it goes away.

Greater roadrunners often build their nest in a thorny bush or a cactus. They line it with leaves, feathers, horse droppings, and even snakeskin.

Fast-Running Birds

26 mph (42 kmph) GREATER ROADRUNNER	30 mph (48 kmph) EMU	43 mph (69 kmph) OSTRICH

Growing Up

A female greater roadrunner usually lays about five eggs over several days. Parents take turns sitting on the eggs. It takes about 20 days for the eggs to hatch. Both parents feed the chicks, which leave the nest about 18 days after hatching. For a few weeks, the young hunt with their parents and are shown how to kill **prey**. Roadrunners are old enough to breed by the time they are two or three years old.

ROADRUNNER FACT

Roadrunner chicks only weigh about **0.5 ounces** (14 g) when they hatch. They grow fast and reach their adult size after just **60 days**.

A Closer Look

Greater roadrunners have **adapted** to their **habitats**. They have unique features that help them survive in their environment.

Wings

A roadrunner's rounded wings are short for its size. The bird can fly briefly to escape **predators** or to get up to a low nest or perch.

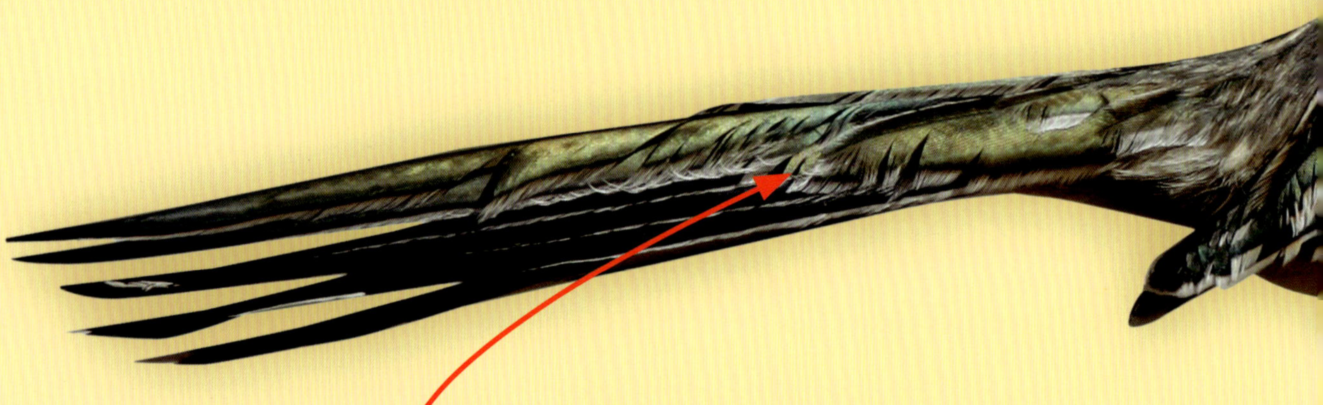

Tail

Roadrunners have dark green and purple tail feathers. These long feathers help the bird stay balanced and steer as it runs.

Nasal Gland

Roadrunners remove unwanted salt from the body through a gland in the nose.

Throat

When it gets too hot, a roadrunner breathes with its mouth open and waggles its throat. This helps it cool down.

Legs and Feet

A roadrunner has long, strong legs and wide feet. This helps it run fast. The bird has four claws on each foot, which leave an X-shaped footprint on the ground.

Communication

Roadrunners, like other cuckoos, are known for their "coo-coo" calls. Male greater roadrunners call loudly from a raised perch. The sound is part of a display that tells other males to stay away. The bird also raises its crest, wags its tail, and shows off the colorful skin near its eyes.

Pairs of birds communicate using different calls. Both males and females make soft single coos and growls. Other sounds include whines, whirs, and clacks. Females also make a barking noise that sounds similar to a coyote's yelp.

A male greater roadrunner will attract a mate by offering food in his beak. He also makes a display of wagging, bowing, and cooing.

Roadrunner

Speeding Up and Steering

Roadrunners can run 20 miles (32 km) per hour for long distances and even faster for brief spurts. They use this speed and short bursts of flight to catch fast-moving prey and escape predators. When running fast, a roadrunner lowers its head and holds its tail in line with the ground. It steers by moving the tail from side to side, not unlike the rudder of a boat.

On cool days, a roadrunner warms up by sunbathing for hours with its back to the Sun.

Roadrunner

Catching Food

A greater roadrunner eats many different small animals, including insects, spiders, scorpions, lizards, and snakes. It eats the eggs of some animals, too. In winter, the bird also eats fruits and seeds. When water is hard to find, roadrunners get all the moisture they need from their food.

A roadrunner hunts on the ground, hiding behind grass and shrubs before running out to snatch prey in its strong, hooked beak. It kills its prey by smashing it against rocks. Then, it swallows smaller prey whole. Large prey take a few gulps to eat.

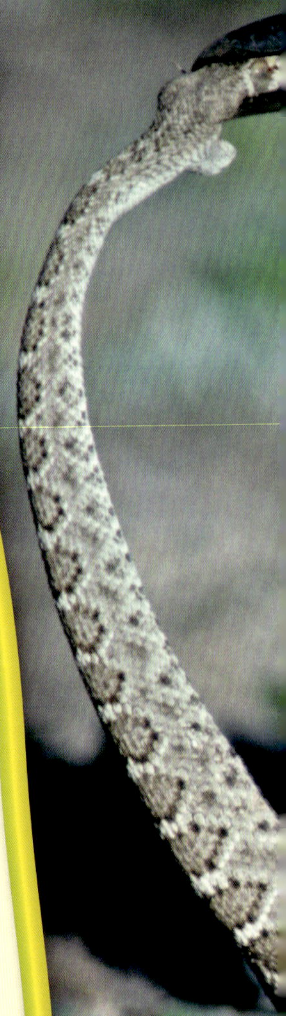

ROADRUNNER FACT

Roadrunners may **work in pairs** to kill large prey, such as a rattlesnake. One distracts the prey, and the other grabs it and smashes it on a rock.

Roadrunner Conservation

Greater roadrunners are not in danger in most places. There are 1.4 million adult birds living in nature. However, in southern California, roadrunner numbers are going down. They are killed by hunters and by some poisonous chemicals used by farmers. The birds' wild habitat is also being replaced by the spread of towns and cities.

Roadrunners can be killed by vehicles as they run across desert roads.

Roadrunner Conservation Status
EX
Extinct
EW
Extinct in the Wild
CR
Critically Endangered
EN
Endangered
VU
Vulnerable
NT
Near Threatened
LC
Least Concern
Lesser Roadrunner
Greater Roadrunner

Roadrunner Quiz

1 Can greater roadrunners fly?

2 How fast can a greater roadrunner run?

3 In which two countries do greater roadrunners live?

4 How many eggs does a female roadrunner lay in a nest?

5 What type of calls are roadrunners and other cuckoos known for?

6 How do roadrunners get moisture when they cannot find water to drink?

7 Where in the United States are roadrunners in danger?

8 How many adult greater roadrunners can be found in nature?

ANSWERS **1.** Yes, but not very well and only for short distances **2.** At speeds of about 26 miles (42 km) per hour **3.** The United States and Mexico **4.** About five eggs **5.** "Coo-coo" calls **6.** From their food **7.** Southern California **8.** 1.4 million

Key Words

adapted: changed to suit the environment

habitats: places where animals live, grow, and raise their young

mated pairs: bonded male and female animals that have young together

predators: animals that hunt other animals for food

prey: animals that are hunted by other animals for food

shrublands: dry areas where only bushes and small trees can grow

species: a group of closely related animals that can reproduce, or have young

territory: the area in which an animal usually lives

Index

Get the best of both worlds.

AV2 bridges the gap between print and digital.

The expandable resources toolbar enables quick access to content including **videos**, **audio**, **activities**, **weblinks**, **slideshows**, **quizzes**, and **key words**.

Animated videos make static images come alive.

Resource icons on each page help readers to further **explore key concepts**.

Published by Lightbox Learning Inc.
276 5th Avenue, Suite 704 #917
New York, NY 10001
Website: www.openlightbox.com

Library of Congress Control Number: 2023944129

ISBN 978-1-7911-5843-9 (hardcover)
ISBN 978-1-7911-5844-6 (softcover)
ISBN 978-1-7911-5845-3 (multi-user eBook)

082023
101122

Printed in Guangzhou, China
1 2 3 4 5 6 7 8 9 0 27 26 25 24 23

Project Coordinator: Priyanka Das
Art Director: Terry Paulhus

Every reasonable effort has been made to trace ownership and to obtain permission to reprint copyright material. The publisher would be pleased to have any errors or omissions brought to its attention so that they may be corrected in subsequent printings.

The publisher acknowledges Alamy, Dreamstime, Getty Images, Minden Pictures, and Shutterstock as its primary image suppliers for this title.